FOOD IN SCHOOLS

BY
TONEY ALLMAN

NORWOODHOUSE PRESS
CHICAGO, ILLINOIS

Norwood House Press
P.O. Box 316598
Chicago, Illinois 60631

For information regarding Norwood House Press, please visit our website at:
www.norwoodhousepress.com or call 866-565-2900.

LIBRARY OF CONGRESS CATALOGING-IN-PUBLICATION DATA

Allman, Toney, author.
  Food in schools / by Toney Allman.
    pages cm. -- (Matters of opinion)
Summary: "Explores the pros and cons of several issues related to food in
the schools, including whether people have the right to eat whatever they
want, and whether the federal government should control what students eat
and weigh. Aligns with Common Core Language Arts Anchor Standards for
Reading Informational Text and Speaking and Listening. Text contains
critical thinking components in regards to social issues and history. Includes bibliography,
glossary, index, and relevant websites"--Provided by publisher.
  Audience: Age 8-12.   Audience: Grade 4 to 6.
  Includes bibliographical references and index.
  ISBN 978-1-59953-604-0 (library edition : alk. paper) -- ISBN 978-1-60357-597-3 (ebook)
1. School children--Food--Juvenile literature. 2. School children--Food--Law and
legislation--United States--Juvenile literature. 3. National school lunch program--Law and
legislation--Juvenile literature. 4. Obesity in children--Juvenile literature. I. Title.
  LB3475.A45 2014
  371.7'160973--dc23
          2013051370

252N—072014
Manufactured in the United States of America in Stevens Point, Wisconsin.

Contents

Note: Words that are **bolded** in the text are defined in the glossary.

Timeline

1894   The first American school lunch program begins in select Boston high schools.

1913   The New York Association for Improving the Condition of the Poor serves 600,000 meals in New York City schools at the cost of one penny each.

1946   The National School Lunch Act becomes a law. It provides low-cost or free lunch for students throughout the United States who are at risk of being undernourished.

1966   The Child Nutrition Act becomes a law. It provides free or low-cost breakfasts to school children in need, as well as free or low-cost milk.

1977   The U.S. General Accounting Office reports that school lunches across the country are often lacking in nutrients and are of portion sizes that may lead to obesity.

1981   The U.S. Congress reduces the amount of money given to schools to pay for lunches but increases the income range for kids to be eligible for free lunches.

1994 Congress passes The School Meals Initiative, requiring school lunches to meet U.S. dietary guidelines. The guidelines limit fat to 30 percent of the calories in the lunch.

2002 Arkansas becomes the first state to pass a law requiring that public schools assess and report BMI data for students.

2010 The Healthy, Hunger-Free Kids Act is signed into law. It is the first major overhaul of nutrition recommendations and requirements for school meals in thirty years.

2012 The nutrition and calorie rules and regulations of the Healthy, Hunger-Free Kids Act go into effect for meals served in school cafeterias throughout the U.S. for the 2012–2013 school year.

2013 The Massachusetts state government passes a law that stops schools from sending BMI assessment letters to the parents of students unless they request the information.

2014 The new rules in the Healthy, Hunger-Free Kids Act limiting the types of foods and snacks sold in school vending machines go into effect for the 2014–2015 school year.

1 What's the Issue With Food and School?

What foods should be available in schools? Should schools care about the eating habits of students? What should those students be eating at school? Who should decide? People have asked these questions since the first national school lunch program began in 1946. In 1966, then president Lyndon B. Johnson said that "good **nutrition** is essential to good learning."[1] The major goal of the school meal programs was to provide **nourishing** meals for students. People also worried that many kids might go hungry while at school. Today, the federal government keeps trying to improve school food programs in the United States. The government grants money to schools for breakfast and lunch programs. It provides guidelines about what kinds of balanced meals should be served to kids at school. Schools that get money from the federal government for the programs have to follow the rules about the kinds of meals served in cafeterias.

In 1965 students are given bag lunches by the National School Lunch program.

The Healthy, Hunger-Free Kids Act

In 2010, President Barack Obama signed a new law with new federal standards and guidelines for cafeteria meals in schools. The law is called the Healthy, Hunger-Free Kids Act (HHFKA). The new rules went into effect on July 1, 2012. Many people believe that the new standards are necessary and important. The old standards

President Barack Obama signs the Healthy, Hunger-Free Kids Act on December 13, 2010.

did not provide the healthiest food choices for students. Hunger is still an important issue in schools. But eating too many **calories** from unhealthy foods is an issue, too. Weighing too much is a serious problem. It can cause health problems, such as **diabetes** and heart disease. It can make it too hard to be physically active. **Obesity** affects many young people.

Many experts say that the U.S. has an obesity epidemic. They say schools are partly to blame. About one out of every three kids in the country is **overweight** or obese.

Some Schools Grow Their Own Food

Every school district in Los Angeles is hoping to establish its own garden to supply cafeterias with fresh, organic vegetables. Although only a few test cases are undergoing the experiment, the results so far have been very promising. Students, faculty, staff, and parents help plant, weed, and harvest the plants. These gardens have both a nutritional benefit as well as a psychological benefit. The vegetables are fresher, eliminate costly transport, and save on higher food costs. The gardens also teach students, many of whom have never had a backyard garden, how to grow plants. Students, who help in the garden as an after-school activity, are gaining pride and a sense of accomplishment by gardening.

The HHFKA could change that. When the law was signed, Tom Vilsack, the U.S. Secretary of Agriculture, said, "Today is a great day for kids throughout our country as they will soon have healthier, and more nutritious food in their schools. As we continue to focus on the twin issues of childhood obesity and hunger, we will increase access to good, quality meals in school cafeterias so the nutritional needs of our youngsters are better met."[2]

A New Way to Eat at School

The HHFKA includes many nutritional rules and meal guidelines. It requires servings of fruits and vegetables every day. It says that students should get less meat than before. The protein foods that are served must be something like lean meat or chicken. A meat alternative, such as a soybean product is also okay. Ground turkey replaces hamburger because turkey is lower in fat. In kindergarten through the fifth grade, the guidelines say that meat servings should be limited to eight to ten ounces per week. Students have to be served fat-free or low-fat milk. Whole milk and 2 percent milk are out. Chocolate milk is out. Starchy foods are limited. White foods such as bread, rice, and potatoes are not okay. The standards suggest whole-wheat breads, brown rice, quinoa, and other whole grains instead. All foods have to be low in sugar and salt. The rules discourage fried or

Whole grains such as the wild rice, quinoa, and brown rice pictured here are replacing less-healthful foods in school cafeterias.

high-fat foods, such as chicken nuggets, pizza, or potato chips. The act also has rules about calories and serving sizes for each meal. For students in elementary schools, lunches can be no more than 650 calories. Students in middle school may have 700 calories. High school students may have 850 calories.

HHFKA's new rules for healthier cafeteria meals, snack bars, and vending machines means big changes for students.

The Healthy, Hunger-Free Kids Act has rules for snack bars and vending machines in schools, too. The standards are called "Smart Snacks in School." They mean no more cookies, candy, donuts, or potato chips. Instead, snacks will be foods like granola bars, fruit cups, and baked tortilla chips. Sodas are banned. Salt, fats, and sugar are limited. Students will not be able to buy unhealthy snacks at all.

The new rules for cafeteria meals, snack bars, and vending machines mean big changes for students. In the U.S., in 2011, 80 percent of middle schools had vending machines. So did 97 percent of high schools. Almost all the vending machines sold treats, not healthy snacks. The treats were not nourishing. Experts say that most treats are "empty calories." They are "junk foods." They taste good, but they do not benefit young bodies. They are full

The Federal School Lunch Program

For many students, the only meal of the day may be the one they eat for school lunch. Millions of children receive a free or low-cost lunch through the National School Lunch Program offered through the United States Department of Agriculture's Food and Nutrition Service. The program also repays schools for offering snacks during after-school activites. All food meets the requirements of the 1995 Dietary Guidelines for Americans. Meals and snacks must offer at least one-third of the recommended dietary allowances of vitamins A and C, protein, iron, calcium, and calories. A child must come from a household with an income at or below 130 percent of the poverty level to qualify for a free lunch. Those whose families earn between 130 percent and 185 percent of the poverty level can receive a lunch for the price of 40 cents or less.

of sugar, salt, and fat. They do not help people to grow or build strong bodies or stay healthy. They can make people gain too much weight. The foods sold in cafeterias were not healthy enough, either. Cafeterias sold hamburgers, hot dogs, french fries, chicken fingers, pizzas, and ice cream. Fruits and vegetables were canned or frozen. Sometimes, they had added sugar and salt. The food was cheap for schools to buy. It was what students wanted to eat. But school lunches were too high in calories. A lot of the choices were junk foods. School breakfasts were not very healthy, either. About half the calories a student eats every day are eaten at school. Many experts worried that school meal choices helped make students obese. Now everything is changed.

Are the Changes Good?

Lots of people are happy about the new rules and changes. Yolanda Gordon is one mother who is pleased. She says, "My son loves it. He loves the sweet potato fries once a week and the broccoli. He says that they eat at school like they eat at home!"[3] Many people, however, do not like all the changes that come with the Healthy, Hunger-Free Kids Act. They do not like schools getting involved

Even with parents and the government involved, students themselves are only likely to eat what they like.

in student health and nutrition. They say that schools are for education, not for worrying about obesity. They do not want the government telling students how to eat or what to eat. Besides, no one can make students eat food if they do not like it. Many students are unhappy. They do not like salad and whole wheat spaghetti for lunch. They do not want a lentil cutlet instead of chicken fingers. Some students say the calorie limits leave them hungry, too. They do not want to buy school lunches anymore.

A Look Inside This Book

The HHFKA has created a lot of controversy. Should schools teach healthy eating habits with their meal and snack programs? Is the government interfering with parents' and kids' rights? Are schools getting involved with student nutrition in the right way? Are the new school food standards going too far? Different people have different reactions to these issues. These issues are complicated. In this book, three of the issues will be covered in more detail: Should people have the right to eat whatever they want? Should the federal government control what students eat? Should schools care about what students weigh? Each chapter ends with a section called **Examine the Opinions**, which highlights one argumentative technique used in the chapter. At the end of the book, students can test their skills at writing their own essay on the book's topic. Finally, notes, glossary, a bibliography, and an index provide additional resources.

2 Should People Have the Right to Eat Whatever They Want?

People have a right to choose what foods they want to eat. Kids should have freedom of choice. Everyone has personal likes and dislikes. Everyone is not the same. No one can force students to eat foods they do not like. Many students like the new foods being served under rules of the Healthy, Hunger-Free Kids Act. But many do not. In Kentucky, students and parents complained to the school board about their new lunch menus. One board member, Myra Mosley, reports, "They say it tastes like vomit."[4]

A mound of trash is displayed in a school cafeteria to show students how much food is wasted.

Kids Have Rights, Too!

Many students around the country just refuse to eat cafeteria food if they dislike it. Some kids stop buying lunch and bring their own lunch from home. Some kids buy lunch and throw away the foods they do not like. Some go hungry because they cannot stand to eat the food they are served. Some kids wait until school is over and go home to fill up on junk food. David R. Just and Brian Wansink are college professors of nutrition. They

Why Kids' Wishes Matter:

David R. Just and Brian Wansink are teachers at Cornell University. They are experts in nutrition. They believe in good nutrition for kids, but they believe in being practical, too. They say that laws cannot change what people like. Lawmakers have to think about "what works and what doesn't." The two experts explain, "Children will choose their food no matter what we place in the lunch line, even if the choice is simply not to eat. If we impose too big a change, kids will simply bring their lunch from home or have pizza delivered at the side door. Or they may skip lunch altogether and wait for an after-school junk food binge.

In an environment where choice rules, we need to make the more healthful choice the more attractive choice, not the only choice."

David R. Just and Brian Wansink, "School Nutrition: A Kid's Right to Choose," *Los Angeles Times*, February 3, 2012.

say, "We cannot simply bully kids into eating healthful foods and take their lunch money."[5] The professors say that kids have rights, too. They say that the new food rules make kids rebel. Students do not get healthier. They do not learn to like healthy foods. Instead, food and money

Student athletes say that they need more calories than the rules allow. They burn up a lot of calories in sports training and exercising.

are wasted as foods are thrown in the garbage. Students should have choices about what foods to eat.

Kids also have the right not to go hungry at school. Some students say they are not getting enough food under the Healthy, Hunger-Free Kids Act. The portion sizes are too small. Student athletes say that they need more calories than the rules allow. They burn up a lot of calories in sports training and exercising. Different people have different kinds of bodies, too. Some are small and do not need many calories. Others are large and need more calories. "One size fits all" is just not true for students.

Ryan Colby is a student in Salt Lake City, Utah. In 2012, he wrote a letter to the local newspaper criticizing the new rules. His letter said:

I am a ninth-grader in the Granite School District. The school last year told us that the school lunch policy would soon change because of the Healthy, Hunger Free Kids Act. I used to always get school lunches. My favorite consisted of a sub sandwich, fruit, a bag of potato chips and milk.

When this act came into place, that all changed. When the policy was implemented, the size of the sandwich decreased, and they excluded the chips and the amount of options of fruit as well. The new version leaves me feeling hungry.

Since the act, I have been bringing lunch every day to school. Decreasing food does not make kids hunger-free.[6]

Many people agree with Ryan. They say the Healthy, Hunger-Free Kids Act is a bad idea. It is not fair to students.

But Not So Fast...

 No: People Should Not Have the Right to Eat Whatever They Want

Do people really have the right to eat whatever they want? Eating a healthy diet is extremely important. Good health for kids is everybody's business in society. People who make bad food choices are unhealthy. Eating junk foods and high-fat, high-sugar foods may cause health problems later in life. Obesity is everyone's problem. People who are overweight can develop diseases such as diabetes or heart problems. Society has to care about helping kids avoid these problems in the future. Obesity can be a killer. Something has to be done about the obesity epidemic. A good place to start is with food in schools.

First Lady Michelle Obama wants to help kids be healthy and fight obesity. She strongly supports the Healthy, Hunger-Free Kids Act. She thinks the issue is not

What students eat is important to their health and therefore important to society.

about students' rights to eat what they want. The issue is about kids' rights to be healthy. It is about parents' rights to teach their kids good eating habits. When the act was signed, Mrs. Obama visited an elementary school in Virginia to explain its benefits. She said, "As parents, we try to prepare decent meals, limit how much junk food our kids eat, and ensure they have a reasonably balanced diet. And when we're putting in all that effort the last thing we want is for our hard work to be undone each day in the school cafeteria."[7] Mrs. Obama does not want schools to sell junk food from vending machines or snack

First Lady Michelle Obama visited an elementary school in Virginia to explain the Healthy, Hunger-Free Kids Act benefits.

bars, either. She wants healthy snacks, no soda vending machines, and healthy breakfasts and lunches.

Lunch at the school when Mrs. Obama visited was ground turkey tacos with cheese, lettuce, and tomatoes; brown rice; fresh fruit; and black bean and corn salad. It

Changing Kids' Diets Will Change Obesity Rates

Retired army generals John M. Shalikashvili and Hugh Shelton argue that the Healthy, Hunger-Free Kids Act will help students become healthy adults:

"Being overweight or obese is the No. 1 medical reason why young men and women are unable to join the military. Research shows that up to 40 percent of what children consume every day takes place during school hours and that 80 percent of children who were overweight between the ages of 10 to 15 were obese by age 25. The final bill [of the HHFK] includes provisions that can get junk food out of schools, nourish more kids who need healthful meals and motivate them and their parents to adopt healthful eating and exercise habits."

John M. Shalikashvili and Hugh Shelton, "President Obama Signs Healthy, Hunger-Free Kids Act of 2010 into Law," www.whitehouse.gov.

was a healthy, low-fat, low-sugar meal, with plenty of fruits and vegetables. Mrs. Obama believes that such lunches are every student's right. She explains, "And let's be clear, this isn't just about our kids' health. Studies have shown that our kids' eating habits can actually affect their academic performance as well…Anyone who works with kids

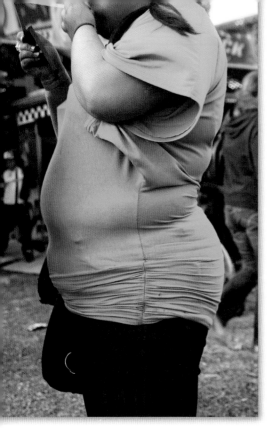

knows that they need something other than chips and soda in their stomachs if they're going to focus on math and science, right? Kids can't be expected to sit still and concentrate when they're on a sugar high, or when they're stuffed with salty, greasy food — or when they're hungry."[8]

Many people believe that students will get used to the new foods and learn to like them. Older students might complain because the food changes are new to them. But young kids will never have eaten anything else at school. They will learn to like healthy foods. The students will develop good eating habits that will last the rest of their lives. They will have more energy. They will do better in school. They will not be at a great risk of obesity. In 2012, a study showed that healthy school foods help fight obesity. The study looked at the weight of 6,300 students in 40 different states. Some states banned junk food in schools. Some states did not. The study followed students in all the states for three years. The kids in the states that banned junk food gained less weight than the kids in the other states.

When schools teach healthy eating habits, everybody wins. Schools should not teach kids bad eating habits. Soda, high-fat foods, and junk food are not rights. Kids have the right to learn to like fresh fruits and vegetables!

Closing Arguments

Many people think that they are in charge of their own food choices. They argue that no one can force them to eat disliked foods. No one should be able to tell them how much to eat at a meal. Others disagree. People who make bad food choices get sick or become obese. The only way to have kids become healthy eaters is to have schools teach them how to eat healthfully and stay well.

Examine the Opinions

Telling the Difference Between Facts and Opinions

Many people love and respect First Lady Michelle Obama. She wants to persuade people that the Healthy, Hunger-Free Kids Act is good for kids. Ryan Colby is just an ordinary student. He wants to persuade people that the HHFKA is not good for kids. His opinion is not the same as Mrs. Obama's. Is he wrong just because he is not an admired, famous person? In logic, the one who holds the opinion has nothing to do with whether the opinion is true.

Good thinkers try to see the difference between opinions and facts. Facts are statements that can be proven to be true. Opinions are about emotions, beliefs, or feelings. They are neither true nor false. People can agree or disagree with opinions. In her statements, Mrs. Obama gives some facts and some opinions. So does Ryan. Try to find examples of both facts and opinions in what they say. Then decide whether you agree or disagree with their ideas about the HHFKA. Are there facts that back up your opinion?

3 Should the Federal Government Control What Students Eat?

👍 Yes: The Government Should Control What Students Eat at School

One of the federal government's most important jobs is to protect **public health**. Some parents fail to provide healthy diets for their children. Some schools do not do a good job with planning meals. Some state governments do not make rules about the foods served in schools. Kids suffer when no one takes charge. Already, the medical costs of illnesses caused by childhood obesity are $10 billion a year. This hurts the sick kids. It hurts society, too. The federal government is supposed to act for the good of society. It should try to protect the health of everyone. Too many kids are overweight but undernourished. Journalist and mother Stephanie Wood

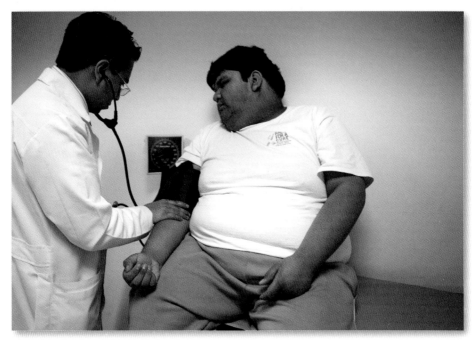

Usually, the food children and teens eat is bought and controlled by parents. Obese teens need the intervention of the government to prevent obesity, many people argue, because parents are not doing their job.

says, "They're not starving for calories; they're starving for nutritious food."[9]

The Government Must Step In

The federal government has the right and duty to protect the health of all American kids. Blanche Lincoln is a senator from Arkansas. She backs the HHFKA. She thinks it is a very good law. In 2010, she said, "The Healthy, Hunger-Free Kids Act will finally put us on a path toward improving the health of the next generation of Americans, providing common-sense solutions to tackling childhood hunger and obesity. This is a resounding victory for our nation's children and an investment that will last a lifetime." Senator Lincoln says that it can be hard for families to pay for healthy foods. She says that healthy foods in schools "will help their children live longer, healthier, more productive lives."[10]

Schools exist to educate their students. The federal government has an interest in good education for all its citizens. Good nutrition should be a part of learning. Students should not be taught to eat unhealthy foods at school. Besides, many schools do not pay for their food programs by themselves. They depend on money from the federal government. The HHFKA gives $4.5 billion to American schools to help them provide meals for students. The government is paying for the meals. So, the government should be able to set the rules about the kinds of foods that are served. That is only fair.

The HHFKA sets strict standards for schools. Maybe, the rules do limit freedom, but the rules are necessary. To

This Is the Government's Job

Richard J. Codey is a former New Jersey governor. He says, "It has always been the role of government to help solve problems, including and especially health crises. Obesity is a health epidemic across our country, and we have a responsibility as a government and a society to do all we can to promote good nutrition and healthy eating so we can reverse this alarming trend." Codey is concerned about public health. He believes that the government should fight obesity in kids. The problem is a big one. It is the government's job to take on big problems. Codey believes the government needs to act for the good of the people.

brainyquote.com

protect public health, the federal government has many laws and rules. Farmers and ranchers, for example, have to follow government rules about the food they grow and sell. The government sets standards about cleanliness, **pesticide** use, and freshness. Nobody objects to those food rules. No one wants to eat tainted food and get sick. A food company has to follow rules about the products it sells. It has to tell the truth about the

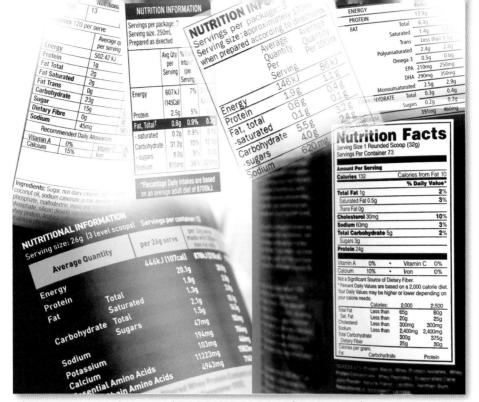

The government has regulations that require food manufacturers to tell the truth about the ingredients that are listed on the package.

ingredients that are listed on the package. A restaurant has to follow food rules, too. It has to keep its kitchen clean and keep bugs and rats out of the building. No one complains about those rules. They protect society. Public health is more important than individual freedom when it comes to food. Public health rules about food in schools protect society, too. The rules keep kids safe from unhealthy diets, obesity, undernourishment, and illness.

But Not So Fast...

No: Government Should Not Control What Students Eat

Public education and schools have always been under local and state control. Parents, communities, and each school decide about what they want to teach kids. They should decide what food is served in schools, too. Cafeterias, snack bars, and vending machines are part of the school. The federal government has no right to tell kids what they should eat at school. Political writer Scott Mayer says, "It's the parents' responsibility, not the federal government's, to make sure their kids eat well at their homes, their friend's houses, their grandparents' houses and at their schools."[11]

Some people argue that the federal government is becoming a "nanny state." A nanny state is a government that tries to protect people all the time. It tries to stop them from making the wrong decisions. It tells them how to behave. It makes many laws to keep people safe. It gives much advice about how people should live their

Ideally, food choices should be made by parents who encourage their children to eat healthy meals.

lives. It makes rules for citizens just like a nanny makes rules for a baby. Congressmen Steve King of Iowa and Tim Huelskamp of Kansas say that the U.S. is becoming a nanny state. They do not like the calorie limits in the HHFKA. They say, "The misguided nanny state, as advanced by Michelle Obama's 'Healthy and Hunger Free Kids Act,' was interpreted...to be a directive that, because some kids are overweight, every child should be put on a diet."[12]

Government control of food in schools just does not work in the real world either. School cafeterias have budgets. They have to be careful how they spend their

Get Out of Our Cafeteria!

John Dively is the head of the Illinois Principals Association. He does not want the federal government to make laws about schools and food. He thinks that school food should be a local issue. The federal government should not tell kids what to eat. He says, "The American education system is designed to give communities control over their schools through local school boards. This principle of local control lies at the root of our democracy. We believe that locally elected school board members are in the best position to make policy decisions that reflect the opinions and needs of their individual communities."

rhetoric.tulane.edu.

money. The federal government does not pay for all the changes ordered by the HHFKA. It gives each school less than a dollar a day per student. Many schools spend more than that to buy food and make school lunches. The schools need the money they get from vending machine sales to make up the difference. If kids stop buying snacks from vending machines, the schools will

Despite the government's best efforts, these students and many others choose pizza over the more healthy food choices at the school cafeteria.

not be able to balance their budgets. If kids refuse to buy the cafeteria meals, the schools will lose money.

In many schools, kids just will not buy or eat the healthy foods. In the state of New York, for example, twelve school districts said that the new lunches were a terrible failure. Tom Pfisterer is the head of food services there. He says, "The guidelines were so prohibitive and restrictive that we lost student customers."[13] The school districts sold a thousand fewer lunches every day because the kids refused to buy them. In Illinois, one school district dropped out of the federal lunch program because the kids just would not buy the lunches. In Texas, a school district dropped the program, too. It was a waste. The kids bought the lunches but threw most of them in the trash. The head of food services in that district is Mary Brunig. She says, "If the children aren't eating the food, there's no nutrition."[14] By 2013, about 200 school districts had opted out of the federal lunch program.

Most schools cannot afford to opt out. They need the federal money to feed their students. In 2013, one government study found that at least 92 percent of school districts are staying with the new program. But that does not mean that kids are getting healthier. It does not mean that kids are really eating the new foods. When the federal government makes rules that are too strict, it does not work. New York educator Christy Multer explains, "Some things you can legislate, and some things maybe you can't legislate. You can't legislate kids to like sweet potatoes."[15]

Closing Arguments

Often, people say that freedom has to be limited to protect public health. Good diets help people live

The HHFKA gives less than a dollar a day to school cafeterias, but this is not enough to cover costs.

long, healthy lives. So, the government has a duty to limit freedom about food choices at school. It needs to guard kids' health. But even if those arguments are true, people do not want a nanny state to make choices for them. The federal government should stay out of it, these critics argue. It is up to families to raise their children in a healthy way.

Examine the Opinions

Name Calling

Propaganda is a message or statement meant to persuade others to believe in a cause or point of view. Propaganda techniques are appeals to a person's emotions. One type of propaganda technique is name calling. Opinions based on name calling do not depend on facts and reasoning. They just depend on labels that sound bad. The label "nanny state" is an emotional appeal. It is an attempt to use name calling to persuade others. Propaganda techniques like this are not about good reasoning. They are an effort to influence feelings. They are words used to persuade people to vote a certain way or buy something or believe in something. As you read about different opinions in this book, you may agree with them. You may disagree. But be aware of the use of name calling as a propaganda technique.

4 Should Schools Care About What Students Weigh?

Obesity and health are serious issues. Controlling what kids eat at school may not be enough to address these issues. After all, kids eat at least half of their meals and snacks outside of school. In nineteen states, state governments have passed laws to help society keep track of student health. Every public school in these states collects data about the height and weight of students. Then, they calculate whether a student is at a healthy weight for his or her age, sex, and height. The math formula used to figure out healthy weight is called the body mass index, or **BMI** for short. BMI is a measure of the percentage of fat in a person's body. If a student has a BMI that is too high, the schools send a

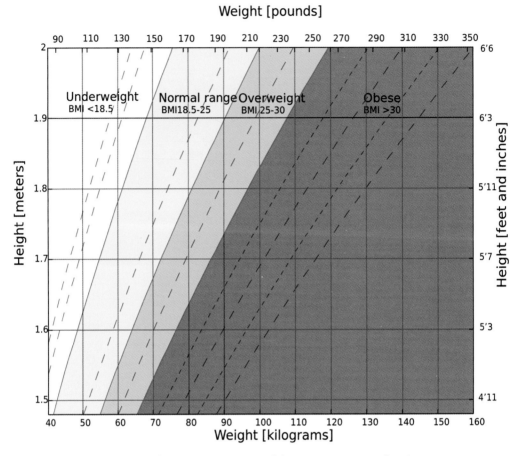

Weight [pounds]

| | 90 | 110 | 130 | 150 | 170 | 190 | 210 | 230 | 250 | 270 | 290 | 310 | 330 | 350 |

Underweight BMI <18.5

Normal range BMI 18.5-25

Overweight BMI 25-30

Obese BMI >30

Height [meters]: 2, 1.9, 1.8, 1.7, 1.6, 1.5

Height [feet and inches]: 6'6, 6'3, 5'11, 5'7, 5'3, 4'11

Weight [kilograms]: 40, 50, 60, 70, 80, 90, 100, 110, 120, 130, 140, 150, 160

BMI is a measure of the percentage of fat in a person's body.

report to the parents. The letter warns that the student may be overweight or obese. It says that the parents should talk about the problem with their doctor. They should think about the child's health and diet. BMI tests are one tool that schools may use to teach good eating habits and improve public health.

The Benefits of BMI Testing:

The American Academy of Pediatrics backs BMI tests in schools. It also likes BMI screening letters. This group of doctors says it is a good idea to warn parents if a child weighs too much. They say that some parents do not know that their kids are overweight. Some do not understand the health risks. A BMI letter could get them to check with their doctor. It could make the family decide to eat a better diet. The academy says, "BMI screening letters are an additional awareness tool to promote conversations about healthy eating habits, exercise, and weight in the safety and confidential environment of the child's home."

Quoted in Maya Rhodan, "Rethinking Public School 'Fat Letters' for Students," *Time Magazine*, September 11, 2013.

BMI Tests Help Kids

The HHFKA says that kids need to learn how to eat healthy diets throughout their lives. BMI tests can help kids know whether they are a healthy weight. The tests might help kids think about the need to change their

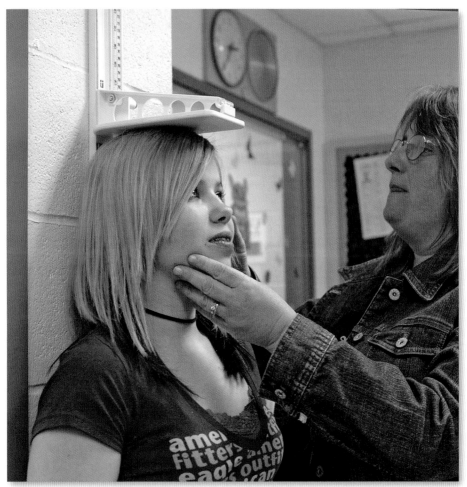

A school nurse gives a physical to a student. Some schools use such physicals to determine students' BMI.

diets. Parents might think about buying healthier foods. The family might learn to change their eating habits. BMI letters to parents are a weapon society can use in the war against obesity. The U.S. Centers for Disease Control and Prevention says that BMI tests in schools help kids. They help society find out how many kids weigh too much. The tests can identify the kids who are in danger because of their weight.

Many doctors say the tests are a good idea, too. Dr. Michael Flaherty worries about kids who weigh too much. He worries that they will grow up to be unhealthy. He believes that BMI testing can improve public health. He says that BMI letters to parents can warn them about a serious health problem. He explains, "The growing number of children and adolescents [teens] seen daily in our clinics with weight management issues, decreased physical activity, and increasing screen time is alarming. Obesity is an epidemic in our country, and one that is compromising the health and life expectancy of our children."[16]

When schools check BMI and report the results to parents, public health can get better. In 2003, Arkansas became the first state to require BMI tests in public schools. It was the first state to send BMI "report cards" to parents. State leaders say that the program has helped them to keep track of obesity in kids. It has made families, schools, and communities more aware of the problem. Health workers collect all the BMI scores from the schools. They use the scores to figure out how many kids are not a healthy weight. The data helps the state know whether programs to fight obesity are working. The state programs include laws that ban junk foods in school vending machines. They include laws that require physical education at school. They use BMI report cards to warn parents if their kids weigh too much. In most of the country, the percentage of kids who are overweight has increased since 2003. In Arkansas, the percentage has stayed the same. This is evidence that BMI reports are helpful to kids.

But Not So Fast...

 No: Schools Should Not Keep Track of What Students Weigh

Some evidence suggests that BMI testing in school is not useful. Math experts say it is not even accurate. The formula for BMI was figured out in 1830, and it has never been changed. Mathematicians say the formula is flawed. Dr. Rexford Ahima of the University of Pennsylvania says, "Most studies depend on BMI, and we know it's not a very accurate measure."[17] BMI tests do not measure how healthy a person is. They cannot measure how big a person's bones are. BMI is just a formula. It cannot even tell the difference between muscle and fat.

BMI scores for athletes are often wrong because they have heavy muscles. The test scores the muscle weight as overweight. Basketball player Michael Jordan, for example, had a high BMI when he was a superstar. Dr. Michael Roizen says, "When he was in his prime, his BMI was 27–29, classifying him as overweight, yet his waist size was less than 30."[18] Jordan was not overweight. The BMI score was wrong. BMI is a quick and easy way to tell whether a person might be overweight or obese. It might work for most people, but it does not work for everyone. It should not be used in schools to label kids as overweight or obese.

An Embarrassing 'Fat Letter'

Ashley-Michelle Papon used to have an eating disorder. She is healthy now, but she remembers how BMI scores can make a person feel fat and ugly. She has studied what scientists say about BMI. She has learned that it has flaws. She is angry that BMI is used to determine normal weight or good health. She calls BMI scores "lies." She explains, "Contrary to what you have probably heard several times over, the BMI is not an accurate indicator of how 'overweight' you are. And it's certainly not a viable indicator of your health."

Ashley-Michelle Papon, "Body of Lies—Debunking the BMI," *Adios Barbie*, May 4, 2011. www.adiosbarbie.com.

BMI report cards do not help kids get healthier. In California, for example, one study found that overweight kids did not lose weight just because their parents got letters. In some schools, only some parents got letters. Other parents did not. Whether or not parents got letters, there was no difference in student weight gain or loss. In Arkansas, parents who got letters did not put their kids on diets. They did not ask their doctors

A teenager with bulimia vomits to keep his weight down. Some school counselors are afraid that a focus on weight may increase eating disorders.

for diet help, either. Not only that, one Arkansas study reported that obese kids were shamed by the BMI tests in their schools.

Many parents and kids call BMI reports "fat letters." Fat letters label kids and make them feel bad about themselves. Fat letters are supposed to be kept private. But often they are not. Other students find out about them. Some kids tease and bully the ones who get fat letters. Lynn Grefe is the president of the National Eating Disorders Association. She thinks the letters are harmful for kids. She says, "It doesn't necessarily lead them to healthier behaviors, but rather among some, it leads to unhealthy behaviors—laxative abuse, purging (vomiting on purpose), excessive over-exercising, dieting—all things that are risky in developing eating disorders...And we have enough eating disorders, we don't need more."[19] Grefe says good health is what matters, not weight.

Quick BMI tests also yield too many mistakes. For example, in October 2013, 11-year-old Lilly Grasso got sent home with a fat letter from her Florida school. It said that Lilly was "at risk" and overweight. Lilly is an athlete. She is 63 inches tall and weighs only 124 pounds. She is healthy and a good weight. Lilly was angry and so were her parents. In Massachusetts, Cameron Watson's parents got a fat letter, too. Cameron is ten years old and a strong athlete. He knew the letter was not true, but his mother worries about other kids in the school. She says they are humiliated, and some are scared to eat all of their lunches at school. She says, "There's much more harm coming from these letters than good."[20]

In October 2013, the Massachusetts state government voted to stop sending the BMI letters home. The schools will still do BMI tests. They will collect the data to help the state keep track of obesity rates. But kids at school will no longer be labeled as overweight or obese. Many people hope that other states will stop sending fat letters, too. Doctors should decide when kids are overweight, not schools.

Closing Arguments:

Many states are very worried about the obesity epidemic among young people. The state governments think that BMI tests at school can help fight the problem. But lots of people do not want schools to keep track of students' weight with BMI tests. They say that the tests are not very accurate. The tests label kids, and the labels are often mistaken. Even accurate BMI tests may do harm. They can scare or shame kids. Many people want schools to stay out of BMI testing.

Examine the Opinions

Examining Evidence

In science, results and conclusions are not the same. Results are what happened in a study. Conclusions are what the scientists think the results mean. The results of the Arkansas study cited in this chapter are facts. Examining an author's evidence is important in determining the strength of his or her argument. A good way to accomplish this is to analyze an author's conclusions. It is a fact that the percentage of overweight students in Arkansas did not increase since 2003. Does this fact mean that BMI reports can help to fight obesity? That conclusion might not be right. Perhaps other things could explain the results. Scientists call those things "variables." One variable was BMI reports. But another variable might have been the ban on junk foods in vending machines. In this study, there is no way to know what variables led to the results. Results are facts, but conclusions are opinions. When you read about a study, try to be aware of the difference between results and conclusions. Ask if the study took all the variables into account. Think about whether the facts back up the opinion.

Wrap It Up!

Write Your Own Essay

In this book the author introduced many differing opinions about the issue of food in schools. These opinions can be used as a launching point to write a short essay on schools and food. Short opinion essays are a common writing form. They are also a good way to use the information presented in this book. The author presented several argumentative techniques and evidence that can be used. In this book, name calling, examining evidence, and telling the difference between facts and opinions were presented as part of the essays to convince you. Any of these techniques could be used to enhance a piece of writing.

There are 6 steps to follow when writing an essay:

Step One: Choose a Topic

When writing your essay, first decide on a topic. As a start you can use one of the three chapter questions from the table of contents in this book.

Step Two: Choose Your Theme

Decide which side of the issue you will take. The first paragraph should state your theme. For example, in an essay titled "Schools Should Not Care What Students Weigh" state your opinion and what action you think should be taken to stop BMI testing and why. You could also use a short anecdote, or story, that proves your point and will interest your reader.

Step Three: Research Your Topic

After choosing your topic, use the materials in this book to write the thesis, or theme, of your essay. You can use the articles and books cited in the notes and also the bibliography. You could also interview people in your life who like or dislike the new school food rules and quote them in your essay.

Step Four: The Body of the Essay

In the next three paragraphs develop this theme. To develop your essay, you should come up with three reasons why BMI testing is wrong. For example, three reasons could be:

- *BMI tests are based on poor math.*
- *BMI testing at school yields too many mistakes.*
- *BMI tests hurt and shame students.*

These three ideas should be developed into three separate paragraphs. Be sure to offer a piece of evidence in each paragraph. Your evidence could be an opinion from a doctor or teacher about the problems with BMI testing. You could also use reports about the harmfulness of fat letters to convince your reader of the urgency of the argument. Each paragraph should end with a transition sentence that sums up the main idea in the paragraph and moves the reader to the next.

Step Five: Write Your Conclusion

The final, or fifth, paragraph should state your conclusion. This should restate your theme and summarize the ideas in your essay. It could also end with an engaging quote or piece of evidence that wraps up your essay.

Step Six: Reread Your Essay

Finally, be sure and reread your essay. Does it have quotes, facts, and/or anecdotes to support the conclusions? Are the ideas clearly presented? Have another reader take a look at your project in order to see if someone else can understand your ideas. Make any changes that you think can help make your essay better.

Congratulations on using the ideas in this book to write a personal essay!

Notes

Chapter 1: What's the Issue with Food and School?

1. Quoted in "Program History and Data," School Nutrition Association. www.schoolnutrition.org/Content.aspx?id=1872.
2. Quoted in The White House, Office of the Press Secretary, "President Obama Signs Healthy, Hunger-Free Kids Act of 2010 into Law," December 13, 2010. www.whitehouse.gov/the-press-office/2010/12/13/president-obama-signs-healthy-hunger-free-kids-act-2010-law.
3. Quoted in Melissa Taylor, "Controversy over School Lunch Foods and Calories," *Class Notes* (blog), Parenting.com, October 9, 2012. www.parenting.com/blogs/mom-congress/controversy-over-school-lunch-foods-and-calories.

Chapter 2: Should People Have the Right to Eat Whatever They Want?

4. Quoted in Cheryl K. Chumley, "Kentucky Kids to First Lady Michelle Obama: Your Food 'Tastes Like Vomit.'" *Washington Times*, August 28, 2013. www.washingtontimes.com/news/2013/aug/28/kentucky-kids-first-lady-your-food-tastes-vomit/.
5. David R. Just and Brian Wansink, "School Nutrition: A Kid's Right to Choose," *Los Angeles Times*, February 3, 2012. articles.latimes.com/2012/feb/03/food/la-oe-just-wansink-a-better-approach-to-healthy-fo-20120203.
6. Ryan Colby, "Letter: 'Hunger Free' Act? Nope," *Deseret News* (Salt Lake City, UT), December 28, 2012. www.deseretnews.com/article/765618833/Hunger-Free-act-Nope.html?pg=all.

7. Quoted in John Rosales, "Healthier Lunches Coming to Schools," *NEA Today*, January 26, 2012. neatoday. org/2012/01/26/healthier-lunches-coming-to-schools/.

8. Quoted in Rosales, "Healthier Lunches Coming to Schools."

Chapter 3: Should the Federal Government Control What Students Eat?

9. Stephanie Wood, "The New American Food Disorder: Overweight and Undernourished Kids," Parenting Advice (blog), Parenting.com, April 10, 2013. www.parenting.com/ blogs/show-and-tell/plum-organics.

10. Quoted in Mary Bruce, "Coming Soon? Healthier School Lunches," ABC News, August 9, 2010. abcnews.go.com/ Politics/healthier-school-lunches-senate-approves-45-billion- bill/story?id=11345256&singlePage=true.

11. Scott Mayer, "Feeding the Nanny-State," Politiseeds.com, February 15, 2012. politiseeds.com/2012/02/15/feeding-the- nanny-state/.

12. Reps. Steve King (R-Iowa) and Tim Huelskamp (R-Kansas), "'Let's Move' Law Is Flawed. "No Hungry Kids Act' Will Fix It," *The Hill's Congress Blog*, September 27, 2012. thehill.com/ blogs/congress-blog/education/258835-lets-move-law-is-flawed- no-hungry-kids-act-will-fix-it.

13. Quoted in Elizabeth Harrington, "USDA Claims Highly Criticized Lunch Standards Are 'Proving Popular,'" The *Washington Free Beacon*, September 18, 2013. freebeacon.com/ usda-claims-lunch-standards-are-proving-popular/.

14. Quoted in Chuck Schechner, "Carroll ISD Opting Out of Federal Lunch Program," CBS DFW News, August 28, 2013. dfw.cbslocal.com/2013/08/28/carroll-isd-opting-out-of-federal-lunch-program/.

15. Quoted in Mary C. Tillotson, "Schools Ditch Federal Lunch Subsidies Due to High Costs," The Heartland Institute, July 29, 2013. news.heartland.org/newspaper-article/2013/07/19/regulations-prompt-schools-ditch-federal-lunch-subsidies.

Chapter 4: Should Schools Care about What Students Weigh?

16. Quoted in Allie Bidwell, "Report: 'Fat Letters' Necessary to Fight Childhood Obesity," *U.S. News and World Report*, August 19, 2013. www.usnews.com/news/articles/2013/08/19/report-fat-letters-necessary-to-fight-childhood-obesity.

17. Quoted in Staff Reporter, "BMI Isn't a Good Indicator of Health Risks," Nature World News, August 24, 2013. www.natureworldnews.com/articles/3645/20130824/bmi-isnt-good-indicator-health-risks.htm.

18. Quoted in Kathleen M. Zelman, MPH, RD, LD, "How Accurate Is Body Mass Index, or BMI?," WebMD, February 12, 2008, p. 2. www.webmd.com/diet/features/how-accurate-body-mass-index-bmi.

19. Quoted in Bidwell, "Massachusetts Schools to Stop Sending 'Fat Letters.'"

20. Quoted in "Beacon Hill Weighs Public Opinion on Student 'Fat Letters,'" CBS Boston, Local News, September 10, 2013. boston.cbslocal.com/2013/09/10/beacon-hill-weighs-public-opinion-on-student-fat-letters/.

Glossary

BMI: Body mass index. A measure of the relative percentage of fat in the body that is based on age, gender, weight, and height and used as an indication of obesity or overweight.

calories: Units of heat that indicate the amount of energy foods will produce in the body.

diabetes: A disease in which there are high levels of sugar, or glucose, in the blood.

nourishing: Containing substances necessary for good health and growth.

nutrition: The process of being nourished by taking in the food that is necessary for health, growth, and good body condition.

obesity: Excessive body fat, usually 20 percent or more than the ideal body weight for an individual.

overweight: More than 10 percent above the ideal weight for an individual.

pesticide: A chemical used to kill pests, such as insects, that harm or damage foods and crops.

propaganda: A message or statement meant to persuade others to believe in a cause or point of view.

public health: The health of the people in general.

Bibliography

Books

Stephen Currie, *Junk Food. Health at Risk series*. Ann Arbor, Michigan: Cherry Lake Publishing, 2014.

Andrea Curtis, *What's For Lunch? How School Children Eat Around the World*. Brighton, MA: Red Deer Press, 2012.

Ursula Furi-Perry, *Constitutional Law for Kids: Discovering the Rights and Privileges Granted by the U.S. Constitution*. Chicago: American Bar Association, 2014.

Rebecca Kajander, C.P.N.P., M.P.H. and Timothy Culbert, M.D., *Be Fit, Be Strong, Be You (Be the Boss of Your Body)*. Minneapolis, MN: Free Spirit Publishing, 2010.

David A. Kessler, M.D., *Your Food Is Fooling You: How Your Brain Is Hijacked by Sugar, Fat and Salt*. New York: Roaring Brook Press, 2013.

Articles

Lauren W., Reno NV, "Junk Food in Schools," Teen Ink (teenink.com/hot_topics/health/article/444802/Junk-Food-in-Schools). The teen author of this article argues that schools should not be so restrictive about junk food in cafeterias and vending machines. She discusses the issues of individual choice, financial considerations, and social attitudes about health.

Websites

BAM! Body and Mind (www.cdc.gov/bam) At this website from the Centers for Disease Control and Prevention (CDC), kids can learn about diet, physical health, diseases, and safety.

Girls Health (www.girlshealth.gov) This website from the U.S. government tells girls, "Be healthy. Be happy. Be you. Beautiful." It discusses healthy eating habits, good body images, physical activity, and coping with illness and disabilities from a girl's point of view.

Kids.Gov (kids.usa.gov) This is the official website for kids by the U.S. government. Visitors can learn about the functions and responsibilities of the federal government, as well as explore the recommendations on health and staying fit.

Kids Health: For Kids (kidshealth.org/kid/index.jsp?tracking=K_Home) In this section of Kids Health.org, young people can read about health and nutrition, calculating BMI, eating disorders, and health problems. There are even recipe links and a medical dictionary.

Kids' World Web Page (www.ncagr.gov/cyber/kidswrld). This site, from the North Carolina Department of Agriculture and Consumer Services, offers much information about nutrition, reading food labels, food safety, and agriculture. It includes games, activities, and quizzes that make the learning fun.

Let's Move! (www.letsmove.gov) Let's Move! Is a program begun by First Lady Michelle Obama to try to solve the problem of childhood obesity within one generation. This is the official website of the initiative. The site includes a special section for kids.

Nourish Interactive (www.nourishinteractive.com). This website is for kids, parents, and educators to learn lots of ways to be healthy and physically fit. It has games to play about nutrition, good recipes, and a nutrition tip of the day.

Nutrition for Kids (www.nutritionforkids.com/kidactivities.htm) This site has games, puzzles, activities, and recipes for kids to learn all about good nutrition.

Index

About the Author

Toney Allman holds degrees from Ohio State University and the University of Hawaii. She currently lives in Virginia, where she enjoys a rural lifestyle, as well as researching and writing about a variety of topics for students.